THE POLITICAL AND ECCLESIAS-
TICAL ALLEGORY OF THE
FIRST BOOK OF THE
FAERIE QUEENE

THE POLITICAL AND ECCLESIAS-TICAL ALLEGORY OF THE FIRST BOOK OF THE FAERIE QUEENE

BY

FREDERICK MORGAN PADELFORD

AMS PRESS
NEW YORK

Reprinted from the edition of 1911, Boston
First AMS EDITION published 1970
Manufactured in the United States of America

Library of Congress Catalogue Card Number: 70-111785
SBN: 404-04856-0

AMS PRESS, INC.
NEW YORK, N. Y. 10003

PREFACE

In this monograph I attempt to elucidate the "dark conceit" of the First Book of Spenser's "Faerie Queene." I was stimulated to undertake this task by the interest which a class of college sophomores took in the poem as a historical document. The members of this class, with Philistine obduracy, frankly refused the *potpourri* of history furnished by the notes in the various editions, and even questioned the introduction of the Spanish Armada into a book that presumably was written some years before the Armada set forth. My interpretation may be wrong, but in these days of higher criticism it is allowed every man to have his say. Of one thing at least I feel sure,—the allegory is in no more parlous state than it was before.

F. M. P.

SEATTLE, WASHINGTON

THE POLITICAL ALLEGORY OF THE FAERIE QUEENE

A century ago Sir Walter Scott, in reviewing Todd's edition of Spenser, offered the following criticism of editors and students of the poet:

> The plan of the Faery Queen is much more involved than appears at first sight to a common reader. Spenser himself has intimated this in his letter to Sir Walter Raleigh prefixed to the poem. For he there mentions, that he has often a general and particular intention, as when he figures, under Gloriana, the general abstract idea of glory, but also the particular living person of Queen Elizabeth. This "continued allegory" or dark conceit, therefore, contains, besides the general allegory or moral, many particular and minute allusions to persons and events in the court of Queen Elizabeth, as well as to points of general history. The ingenuity of a commentator would have been most usefully employed in decyphering what, "for avoiding of jealous opinions and misconstructions," our author did not choose to leave too open to the contemporary reader. But although everything belonging to the reign of the Virgin Queen carries with it a secret charm to Englishmen, no commentator of the Faery Queen has taken the trouble to go very deep into those annals, for the purpose of illustrating the secret, and, as it were, esoteric allusions of Spenser's poem.[1]

Were Scott writing to-day, his criticism would be almost as pertinent as it was in 1805, for during the past century English scholars have left this absorbing problem almost untouched. One contribution of moment, and only one, has been made. In 1888 Mr. J. Ernest Whitney

[1] *Edinburgh Review*, Vol. VII (Oct. 1805), p. 214.

presented a paper before the American Philological Association, in which he elaborated the theory that there is a general correspondence between the events of the First Book and the progress of the Reformation in England.[1]

The suggestion for such a thesis had previously been made by Upton, — an editor still deserving to be ranked as one of the foremost of the interpreters of Spenser, — who proposed that the Red Cross Knight might be identical with Henry VIII, as *Defensor Fidei;* but it remained for Whitney to demonstrate the reasonableness of this proposal.[2] Whitney surveyed the book as a whole, and saw its general significance, but, aside from incorporating a few of the chance suggestions of earlier scholars, he did not attempt to identify the various personages of the romance with actual historical characters, or to connect the detailed episodes of the cantos with the actual events of history. Perhaps he was wise in abandoning the problem at this point, for one must needs feel apprehensive of results when dealing with a question that must always remain more or less in the realm of conjecture. Yet, if we are ever to discover the deeper meaning of this allegory, some one must launch boldly, if rashly, forth. Accordingly I have made a venture at the somewhat detailed interpretation of parts of this First Book. In some of my conclusions I confess to a tolerable degree of confidence; and I comfort myself with the reflection that even if other scholars cannot agree with my findings, I have yet reintroduced an important question into the forum of letters.

[1] *Transactions of the American Philological Association*, Vol. XIX, p. 40.
[2] Mention should be made of the dissertation by Max Hoffmann, "Über die Allegorie in Spensers Faerie Queene" [Königsberg], in which this suggestion receives slight consideration.

That the "Faerie Queene" allows of historical interpretation — indeed, that the author regarded the historical aspect as intrinsic — is abundantly evident from his own words. In the letter to Sir Walter Raleigh he specifically states that the allegory shadows forth real events and persons, and gives a clue to the interpretation by identifying Queen Elizabeth with the Faerie Queene in her aspect as queen, and with Belphœbe in her aspect as a "vertuous and beautifull Lady." In the prologue to the First Book, which really serves as a prologue to the entire poem, the poet appeals to Clio, the muse of history, rather than to Calliope, the muse of epic poetry, — a choice that was not due to error, as some scholars have suggested, but that was dictated by the main design of the poem. In the opening stanzas of the Second Book, Elizabeth is told that "in this antique ymage" she may see her "great auncestry," and a hint is given the reader that the allegory, though designedly occult, allows of interpretation:

> Of Faerie Lond yet if he more inquire,
> By certain signes, here sett in sondry place,
> He may it find: ne let him then admire,
> But yield his sence to bee too blunt and bace,
> That note without an hound fine footing trace.

It is indeed a question if Spenser did not attempt a minuteness of historical delineation that proved increasingly burdensome as the work progressed, and that required simplification of the original design; there would seem to be a hint of such a change in the closing stanza of the opening book, when the poet complains that

> We must land some of our passengers
> And light this weary vessel of her lode.

Our present knowledge of the poem, however, does not allow a conclusive answer to this question.

If this book is to be examined as allegorical church history, it will be well first to determine Spenser's ecclesiastical sympathies as they may be deduced from sources outside of the book itself. Spenser came from a family of pronounced Protestant, as opposed to Roman Catholic, sympathies.[1] Among the earliest and most vivid of his memories must have been the Protestant martyrdoms at Smithfield; for the poet was born at East Smithfield, in 1552(?), and the persecutions of Mary began in 1555 and claimed nearly three hundred victims before her death in 1558. The sensitive mind of the child must have been deeply impressed with these horrors. He was certainly old enough to feel the wave of relief at Mary's death and to catch the spirit of Protestant rejoicing when Elizabeth kissed the Bible presented her by the nobles at her entry to London, and promised "diligently to read therein!" As a youth he doubtless pored over Foxe's great work, the "Actes and Monuments," which was the sole authority for church history in Protestant households and an armory of arguments in defense of Protestantism against Catholicism[2]; a book which was so eagerly sought that three editions had appeared before the poet, at the age of twenty-seven, completed the "Shepheardes Calender" and began the composition of the great poem which was to be the supreme exponent of his ideals.[3]

[1] Cf. Grosart, "The Ancestry and Family of Spenser," Works of Spenser, Vol. I.
[2] Dictionary of National Biography, Vol. VII (ed. of 1908), p. 588.
[3] On Oct. 5, 1579, Spenser wrote to Gabriel Harvey: "I wil in hand forthwith with my 'Faerie Queene,' whyche I praye you hastily send me with al expedition." On the 23d, Harvey replied: "In good faith I had once again well nigh forgotten your 'Faerie Queene'; howbeit by good chance I have now sent her home at the last, neither in better nor worse case than I found her." D. N. B., Vol. XVIII, p. 796.

As a very young man he showed his ecclesiastical predilections in the "Shepheardes Calender," for the eclogues for May, July, and September discuss the conditions of the Church and the evils of the papacy. In the eclogue for May, Palinode argues in defense of worldliness in the clergy, whereas Piers pleads for a humble, devout priesthood. E. K., who supplies the argument and the glossary, and who must have been intimately acquainted with Spenser's views,[1] says that this eclogue contrasts the Protestant and the Catholic clergy, and explains the story of the kid and the fox with which the eclogue closes as "the simple sorte of the faythfull and true Christians" deceived by "the false and faithlesse Papistes." The eclogue for July, in the words of the argument, " is made in the honour and commendation of good shepheardes, and to the shame and disprayse of proude and ambitious Pastours." It pleads for the devotion and simplicity of the early shepherds, condemns the "purple and pall," and concludes with a description of the corrupt practices of Rome. In both this and the preceding eclogue Archbishop Grindal, under the name of Algrind, is extolled as the ideal Churchman both in doctrine and in life. In the eclogue for September, Diggon Davie[2] discourses to Hobbinol[3] on the abuses and loose living of popish prelates, their greed and lust, and on the cunning of the wolves and foxes who often outwit the unwary shepherd.

[1] For the present purpose, it is immaterial whether " E. K." is the poet himself, his friend Edward Kirke, or, as Professor Fletcher suggests, the two acting jointly.
[2] Grosart would identify this character with Spenser's Brabantine friend, Johan Vander Noodt, who sought refuge in England "as well for that I would not beholde the abominations of the Romyshe Antechrist as to escape the handes of the bloudthirsty." Works of Spenser, Vol. I, pp. 25-28.
[3] Gabriel Harvey.

The Protestant literature of the time is full of such pictures of the corruption at Rome,[1] and such comparisons of the papal prelates to foxes and wolves.[2] Spenser was clearly Protestant, as opposed to Roman Catholic, in his feelings.

But it is not enough to show that Spenser was a so-called Protestant, for, as in our own day, there were all degrees of protestation, from the noisy, wrangling Puritan who would sweep away every vestige of the historic Church, to the High Churchman who sympathized with most of the practices of the Church as they existed prior to the Reformation, and who was quietly working to reestablish much of the elaborateness of early usage. Nor is it sufficient to show that Spenser was a Puritan, for here again the latitude of the term allows of misunderstanding. In a sense Bishop Cox was a Puritan, but he did not hesitate to class the more destructive wing of the Puritan party along with the Papists as very Antichrist.[3] Where in the Protestant and Puritan movements is Spenser to be placed? If he lauds both the life and teachings of Grindal, is it not reasonable to suppose that

---

[1] Cf. Philpot, Examinations and Writings, pp. 389, 418; Jewel, Works, Vol. II, pp. 707, 728, 807; Vol. IV, pp. 627, 644, 745; Hooper, Early Writings, p. 447; Ridley, Works, p. 53; Cranmer, Works, Vol. II, p. 63: " Of the prosperity and security that the false church hath in worldly pleasures, using the same with all greediness and voluptuousness of carnal lusts, with the wicked devices of tyranny against Christ and his true members, . . . it is most plainly written in the second and third chapters of the Book of Wisdom ";— all in the publications of the Parker Society.

[2] Cf. Zurich Letters, Vol. I, p. 322, and Sandys, Sermons, p. 397 [Parker Society].

[3] Zurich Letters, Vol. I, p. 309: " But the strength of the Lord and his strong tower have hitherto defended us; and the Lord will defend his own even to the end, in spite of the chafing and assaults of those two antichrists."

Grindal's attitude fairly represents his own? Now Grindal was a Puritan in the sense that he advocated devout and humble living, and simplicity and sincerity of worship,—the sense in which the most intelligent and spiritual members of the Established Church were Puritans,— but he had no sympathy with the rancorous and violent spirit of those extremists who sought to overthrow the episcopal system and to rob the service of form and dignity by degrading the ritual, — men who would snatch the very vestments from the backs of the clergy. His temper is well illustrated in the following excerpt from a letter written to Henry Bullinger in 1573:

> Our affairs, after the settlement of the controversy respecting ceremonies, were for some time very quiet: when some virulent pamphlets came forth, privately printed, contrary to law, in which almost the whole external polity of our Church was attacked. For they maintain that archbishops and bishops should altogether be reduced to the ranks; that the ministers of the Church ought to be elected solely by the people; that they ought all to be placed upon an equality; . . . (they state) that the Church of England has scarcely the appearance of a Christian Church, — that no set form of prayer ought to be prescribed, but that in the holy assemblies each minister should pray as the Holy Ghost may dictate; that the infants of popish recusants, as far as the use of baptism is concerned, are unclean (I use their own words). . . . But a royal edict was lately published, in which libels of this sort are forbidden to be circulated for the future; which circumstance, as I hope, will retard their endeavours. They are young men who disseminate these opinions, and they have their supporters, especially among those who are gaping for ecclesiastical property.[1]

Again, writing to Rudolph Gualter, he thus characterizes the Puritan agitators:

> You candidly and truly confess, Master Gualter, that there are some among those brethren who are a little morose; and you might

[1] Zurich Letters, Vol. I, p. 292.

add too, obstreperous, contentious, rending asunder the unity of a well-constituted Church, and everywhere handing up and down among the people a form of divine worship concocted out of their own heads; that book, in the meantime, composed by godly fathers, and set forth by lawful authority, being altogether despised and trodden under foot. In addition to this, they inveigh in their sermons, which are of too popular a character, against the popish filth and the monstrous habits, which, they exclaim, are the ministers of impiety and eternal damnation. Nothing moves them, neither the authority of the state, nor of our Church, nor of her most serene majesty, nor of brotherly warning, nor of pious exhortation. Neither have they any regard to our weaker brethren, who are hitherto smoking like flax, but endeavour dangerously to inflame their minds. ... We are undeservedly branded with the accusation of not having performed our duty, because we do not defend the cause of those whom we regard as disturbers of peace and religion; and who by the vehemence of their harangues have so maddened the wretched multitude, and driven some of them to that pitch of frenzy, that they now obstinately refuse to enter our churches, either to baptize their children, or to partake of the Lord's supper, or to hear sermons. They are entirely separated both from us and from those good brethren of ours; they seek bye paths; they establish a private religion, and assemble in private houses, and there perform their sacred rites, as the Donatists of old, and the Anabaptists now; and as also our papists, who run up and down the cities that they may somewhere or other hear mass in private.[1]

Such was the attitude of Archbishop Grindal. In the parlance of to-day, Grindal was not a dissenter, but a Low Churchman, and the presumption is that Spenser, who expressed such warm admiration for him, was of the same school. Moreover, Spenser has, I believe, paraded the vociferousness of the more turbulent Puritans, and given his own rebuke to men who had no regard for things of sacred and historic association, in the Blatant Beast, the

---

[1] Zurich Letters, Vol. I, p. 237. Cf. also Horn's letter to Bullinger under date of Aug. 8, 1571, ibid. p. 249, and Strype, Life of Grindal, p. 439, et freq.

personification of scandal or calumny. The conclusion of the career of the Blatant Beast is thus described :

> From thence into the sacred Church he broke,
> And robd the Chancell, and the deskes downe threw,
> And Altars fouled, and blasphemy spoke,
> And th' Images for all their goodly hew,
> Did cast to ground, whilest none was them to rew;
> So all confounded and disordered there.[1]

Upton[2] construes this passage to mean that the Roman Catholic priests turned the Church to mercenary account and preached scandal from its pulpit; but clearly the scandal is directed *against* the Church, and the scandal-mongers are those who seek to tear down chancel, desk, and altar. Surely Spenser must have had in mind those obnoxious malcontents who could not rest so long as the Church retained any of its ancient aspect,— the class of men who strove to remove the very fonts and eagles from the sanctuary.[3] Through this character Spenser but gives poetical utterance to a feeling that was general among the supporters of the Established Church, and that finds frequent and anxious expression in the ecclesiastical correspondence of the time.[4] Certainly there were those among Spenser's contemporaries who identified the Blatant Beast with the Puritans, for Ben Jonson remarked on this very point to William of Hawthornden.[5]

[1] Faerie Queene, 6. 12. 25.   [2] Spenser's F. Q. Vol. II, p. 656.
[3] Parker, Correspondence, p. 450 [Parker Society].
[4] Cf. Zurich Letters, Vol. I, pp. 287, 295; and the General Index of the publications of the Parker Society.
[5] Works of William Drummond of Hawthornden [Edinburgh, 1711], p. 225: "Spenser's stanzas pleased him [Jonson] not, nor his matter. The meaning of the allegory of his Fairy Queen he had delivered in writing to Sir Walter Raleigh, which was 'that by the Bleating Beast he understood the Puritans, and by the false Duessa the Queen of Scots.'"

In the "Cantos of Mutabilitie"[1] occurs another apparent reference to the Puritans:

> And backward yode, as Bargemen wont to fare
> Bending their force contrary to their face;
> Like that ungracious crew which faines demurest grace.

There was no other class in English society to whom this could apply. Again, the abstemious and disagreeable Elissa, the elder sister of Medina,[2] is an extreme Puritan type. Just as Sir Guyon chose Medina, the golden mean, in preference to the prudish Elissa and the wanton Perissa, so Spenser chose the golden mean between the self-righteous and barren Puritan and the sensuous Roman Catholic. Medina,

> A sober sad and comely courteous Dame;
> Who rich arayd, and yet in modest guize,
> In goodly garments that her well became,
> Fayre marching forth in honorable wize.[3]

expresses very well the temper of the Low Churchman in the days of Elizabeth.

Indeed, the preference for the golden mean, thus allegorically expressed, is supremely characteristic of Spenser. It led him, in "Mother Hubberd's Tale,"[4] to condemn mumming, masking, dice, cards, and courtezans, and at the same time to commend feats of strength, such as running, hunting, and wrestling, and to picture the courtly gentleman as recovering the joy of youth with music and "ladies gentle sportes." It gave him sympathies both spiritual and sensuous; both medieval, and humanistic and Italian; both

---

[1] F. Q. 7. 7. 35. 7–9. Cf. Warton's note, Todd, Works of Edmund Spenser, Vol. VII, pp. 229–230.
[2] F. Q. 2. 2. 35.   [3] Ibid. 2. 2. 14. 5–8.   [4] ll. 717–758.

Catholic and Protestant; both Hellenic and Hebraic. His philosophy was a felicitous blending of Puritanism and Platonism, which enabled him to maintain a balance between the things of the flesh and the things of the spirit, and between the beautiful and the good. As the most careful student of his philosophy has written:

> Spenser's Puritanism saved him from seizing upon those pagan and sensuous elements in classical literature which proved a pitfall to so many of his contemporaries; it made him blind to the more dangerous aspects of Platonism and helped to concentrate his attention on that which is noblest and most characteristic in Plato, — his ethical genius; on the other hand Spenser's Platonism preserved him from the, artistically at any rate, no less dangerous pitfalls of Puritanism; it helped to preserve him from mental narrowness by showing him the best possible examples of freedom and flexibility of mind, and taught him what, as a poet, it was most essential he should know, — that beauty is not only consistent with moral earnestness but may be made to contribute to it in the most powerful way.[1]

I have thus gone into detail in trying to determine Spenser's attitude on ecclesiastical matters because it has an intimate bearing on the interpretation of the allegory of the First Book.[2]

In offering my interpretation I shall not invariably proceed according to the strict sequence of the story, but I shall try to find the interpretation of some of the less difficult phases of the allegory, and proceed from these to the consideration of the more difficult. It will of course be necessary to tell the story somewhat in detail, in order that the discussion may be clear.

[1] Lilian Winstanley, Edmund Spenser: The Fowre Hymnes, p. xi.
[2] For an elaborate discussion of Spenser's theology as essentially Calvinistic, see the article by Lilian Winstanley in *Modern Language Quarterly*, Vol. III, no. 6, p. 103.

The opening stanzas of Canto I introduce the knight and lady who are the hero and heroine of the book, and their attendant dwarf:

> A gentle Knight was pricking on the plaine,
> Ycladd in mightie armes and silver shielde,
> Wherein old dints of deepe woundes did remaine,
> The cruell markes of many'a bloody fielde;
> Yet armes till that time did he never wield.
> His angry steede did chide his foming bitt,
> As much disdayning to the curbe to yield:
> Full jolly knight he seemd, and faire did sitt,
> As one for knightly giusts and fierce encounters fitt.
>
> And on his brest a bloodie Crosse he bore,
> The deare remembrance of his dying Lord,
> For whose sweete sake that glorious badge he wore,
> And dead, as living, ever him ador'd:
> Upon his shield the like was also scor'd,
> For soveraine hope which in his helpe he had.
> Right faithfull true he was in deede and word,
> But of his cheere did seeme too solemne sad;
> Yet nothing did he dread, but ever was ydrad.
>
> . . . .
>
> A lovely Ladie rode him faire beside,
> Upon a lowly Asse more white then snow,
> Yet she much whiter; but the same did hide
> Under a vele, that wimpled was full low;
> And over all a blacke stole she did throw:
> As one that inly mournd, so was she sad,
> And heavie sate upon her palfrey slow;
> Seemed in heart some hidden care she had,
> And by her in a line a milke-white lambe she lad.
>
> So pure and innocent, as that same lambe,
> She was in life and every vertuous lore;
> And by descent from Royall lynage came
> Of ancient Kings and Queenes, that had of yore

Their scepters stretcht from East to Westerne shore,
And all the world in their subjection held;
Till that infernall feend with foule uprore
Forwasted all their land, and them expeld;
Whom to avenge, she had this Knight from far compeld.

Behind her farre away a Dwarfe did lag,
That lasie seemd, in being ever last,
Or wearied with bearing of her bag
Of needments at his backe. . . .

Thus, as they journey, a sudden storm breaks overhead, and they take refuge in a dense wood, whose thickset trees shut out the light of heaven. Admiring the trees and "joying to heare the birdes sweete harmony," they wander deeper into the forest, until, the storm over and wishing to retrace their steps, they find that they are lost. So many paths confront them that at first they are at a loss which to choose, but finally elect the one that seems most traveled. This brings them to a cave. The knight quickly dismounts, hands his "needlesse spere" to his dwarf, and makes for the entrance. Nor, like the "fearefull Dwarfe," is he deterred by his lady's warning that this den is the abode of "Errour." Entered within the "darksome hole," lo! a monster, half serpent and half woman, surrounded by her thousand young, which, taking fright, creep into their dam's mouth. Thereupon ensues a fierce conflict, in which, trusting to his "trenchand blade" and his shield, the knight comes off victor; only, however, after the beast has almost wrested his shield from his hand and the lady has warned him to add faith unto his force. Thence the travelers set out again, and towards evening fall in with one Archimago, an aged man, clad as a monk, whom the knight takes for a palmer. The meek behavior of the stranger wins the confidence of the knight, and he accepts the proffered shelter of a hermitage. His guests retired, the old man seeks his study and his magic books, and secures the services of an "ydle dream," wherewith the cunning hypocrite tempts the chastity of the virgin knight. But the knight withstands the temptation. Failing in this attempt, Archimago next contrives a show of Una lying in the embrace of a fair young squire. The knight beholds the spectacle, is convinced of the impurity of his lady, and with his dwarf flees. Una in turn awakes, finds her knight departed, and sorrowfully sets out in search of him. The knight at length chances to meet a faithless Saracen, Sansfoy, attended by a lady of seeming fairness. The men do battle and Sansfoy is slain. Thereupon the lady, who is in reality the false Duessa, attaches herself to the knight, and by fair words deceives him, pretending that she is faithfulness itself, a maid by name Fidessa. The unsuspecting knight takes her to be "the fairest wight that lived yet." Thence setting forth, they wander for a time, and at length seek rest beneath shady trees. On breaking a bough, the knight discovers that the trees are two lovers, Fradubio and Frælissa, whom Duessa had thus cruelly imprisoned. Fradubio tells his melancholy story. Once, riding with his lady, he met a false knight with a fair companion. She was of seeming loveliness, though she later proved to be the false Duessa. Dispute arising as to which lady was the fairer, the false knight was overthrown, and Fradubio thus became the protector of the two. One day he

> cast for to compare
> Whether in beauties glorie did exceed,

and then, fearfull lest she lose, the enchantress Duessa made her rival to appear of "foule ugly forme" and left her to turn to a moldering tree. So Fradubio took Duessa for his dame. But one day he "chaunst to see her in proper hew," a "filthy foule old woman"; and Duessa saw his ill-concealed disgust and likewise transformed him into a tree, to stand beside his former love. This evil plight they could never change till bathed in a living well. Such is the somber tale, but the knight is too insensible to detect therein the image of his own conduct, and, placing Duessa on her steed, proceeds on his way. Such is the story of the first two cantos.

After giving a digest of the entire book to show how all the episodes hinge upon the thought of the defense of the faith, Whitney thus begins the interpretation of the historical or personal allegory, which he believes to be the one "continued allegory":

Henry VIII. came to the throne of England in 1509. Luther nailed his ninety-five theses to the door of the Wittenberg Castle Church on All Saints' eve, 1517. Before the death of his elder brother, Henry VIII. had been educated for the Church. Deeply interested in the Renaissance he was still more interested in the Reformation. In the eleventh year of Henry's reign, in October, 1520, Luther published the most important work of the times, "The Babylonian Captivity of the Church of God." To this the royal theologian of England made reply with a book called "*Assertio septem sacramentorum adversus Martinum Lutherum.*" Regarding this book a recent Roman Catholic authority has written: "We know of none among the contemporary works which defend the Church more filially and more warmly." For this enthusiastic defense, in the following year, 1521, Pope Leo X. conferred upon Henry the title "*Fidei Defensor,*" and commanded all Christians so to address him. The title has been held by the sovereigns of England to this day. Pope Clement VII. confirmed the title. In 1527, Protestants were still persecuted in England, but Henry had resolved on the divorce, which led to such important results. In 1531 the king was acknowledged supreme head of the Church of England. In 1532 Anne Boleyn was crowned. In 1534 the Act of Supremacy was passed. From that time on, the former defender of the Roman faith became its oppressor and the champion and defender of the Protestant faith. Henceforward, except in the reign of Mary, whenever an English sovereign used the title "*Fidei Defensor*," the implied adjective was wholly different in significance from the one in the minds of Popes Leo X. and Clement VII.

Now let us see what use Spenser made of this material. St. George is *Fidei Defensor* not representing Henry VIII. alone, but rather the sovereigns of England, who bear the title of Defender of the Faith. With the just license of a patriotic poet, Spenser represents Una, or the cause of truth, as the peculiar charge of St. George, or England. At the beginning of the allegory the tempest of the Reformation drives the wandering pair into a labyrinth of Error, and there St. George fights sturdily against the Dragon Error in defense of Truth and Faith. Perhaps never in all Christian history has this error been so common, so excusable. In spite of his theological training, or possibly because of it, to Henry VIII., as to nearly all Englishmen, the true faith seemed at first to be that which every Christian sought in the Church of Rome. Even Luther was a devoted Papist before he became a devoted Reformer.

Throughout the first of the allegory Una is veiled to her lover, and we see the significance of that puzzling mystery. The Dragon of the Wood of Error was a veritable dragon, and in attacking it, St. George was the champion of no false faith, but simply struggling with misunderstanding. Una typifies the true Christian Church on earth, long represented by Rome only, from this time forward represented, though still half concealed under her black stole, by the Protestant Church only. She is that heavenly truth which Luther sought first in Rome, which England at the beginning of the Reformation still seemed to see in Rome, and St. George is her champion. Archimago, symbol of papal influence, by lies and delusions, convinces St. George that his veiled Una is not truth, but foulest falsehood. The meaning is, that before England found its way out of the great tangle of error, it was led to turn from the true faith as St. George abandoned Una.

We next find the King of England defending the false faith, as St. George becomes the defender of Fidessa not knowing that she is the falsely faithless Duessa. But in this very change St. George gives the death blow to Sansfoy, the faithless, and becomes Fidessa's sole defender. In much the same way England sought to defend the island faith from injury by making Henry supreme head of the Church in England, and thus gave a far heavier blow than was intended to the old established papal faith on the island. I think, too, that in the relations of Duessa and the Red Cross Knight there is much more than a shadowy fabric of allusion to Henry VIII.'s favor shown to certain less substantial phases of the Renaissance, which might well be represented by the oriental Duessa, the daughter of the emperor of the West, and the link between Constantinople and Rome.[1]

The Red Cross Knight, according to Spenser's own testimony, is St. George, which is England as a militant spiritual force ; and as the sovereign, the Defender of the Faith, was the concrete embodiment of this force, I agree with Whitney that the Red Cross Knight and Henry VIII are to an extent to be identified. Una, I also take to be truth as ultimately revealed in the doctrines and practices of the liberated and purified national Church. Thus to assist the spirit of truth completely to possess the Church, thus to define and illustrate Christ's ideal for the Church, was the exalted and peculiar office of England among the nations.

In the main, therefore, I believe that Whitney's interpretation is correct ; I shall try to add to it, however, and in some respects to modify it, after discussing the third canto.

In Canto III, Una, "forsaken, wofull, solitarie," wanders in quest of her knight. One day as she is resting in a grove, a "ramping Lyon ... hunting full greedy after salvage blood," bursts out of the thick wood and makes to

[1] *Transactions of the American Philological Association*, Vol. XIX, p. 62.

devour her. But when he draws nigh, his fierceness is suddenly changed to fawning, and when she mounts her "snowy Palfrey" he becomes her attendant. Long they travel thus, until at length she spies a damsel bearing on her shoulders a pot of water. Una accosts her, asking for shelter, but the damsel's only answer is to throw down her pitcher and run away. The travelers, however, follow her and seek admittance to the house in which she has taken refuge. When no response is made, the lion breaks open the door, discovering the damsel and her blind mother crouching in the corner. In the darkness of this room the old woman is wont to say

> Nine hundred *Pater Nosters* every day
> And thrise nine hundred *Aves*,

and to do penance in ashes and sackcloth. At night Una lies down to rest, the lion at her feet. Suddenly there is knocking at the door, and when the women, fearful of the lion, fail to open it, with curses a man, carrying a heavy load on his back, breaks in the door. The lion straightway leaps upon him and kills him, rending him in a thousand pieces, while "the thirsty land dronke up his life." This man was a stout and sturdy thief,

> Wont to robbe churches of their ornaments,
> And poore mens boxes of their due reliefe,

and to bestow his pilfered treasures on the damsel, who was his paramour. With morning, Una and the lion depart, followed afar by the "fearful twayne" who lament and curse her. Thus cursing, they are met by the subtle Archimago, who has deceitfully clad himself in armor like to that of the Red Cross Knight. Learning of Una's whereabouts, he follows and overtakes her, and she is rejoiced to recover her supposed lord. They ride but a little way when they see a stern knight, strongly armed and mounted on a fierce steed, pricking toward them. It is Sansloy. Eager to avenge the death of Sansfoy, his brother, he engages Archimago, little used to arms, and quickly unhorses him. But when, "rending up his helmet," he discovers the visage of Archimago, he learns too late that he has struck a friend. Thinking that Archimago is dead, he next turns to Una and rudely seizes her. Thereupon the lion leaps upon him, but Sansloy is too much for his assailant, and kills the faithful beast and carries Una away.

It is of course the suppression of the monasteries that is described in the first part of this canto. The old hag symbolizes superstition; her licentious daughter, fearful of the truth, the immorality of the monks; and the robber, monastic greed and rapine.[1] The lion is identified by most editors, who follow the suggestion of Upton,[2] with Henry VIII. But clearly Henry cannot fill the rôle both of the Red Cross Knight and of the lion, for the lion assumes the protection of Una when the Red Cross Knight deserts her. Moreover, the lion is killed by his adversary and disappears from the poem, so that if the lion is Henry, the death of the lion at the hands of Sansloy cannot refer to physical death, in which case the allegory must be interpreted in some such general way as that Henry was overcome by the spirit of lawlessness. But even so, one would expect to have the lion taken captive by his conqueror and made his subject, rather than killed by him. Moreover, if Sansloy stands for the spirit of lawlessness, Sansfoy

[1] Cf. Works of Bishop Ridley, p. 402 [Parker Society].
[2] Spenser's F. Q. Vol. II, p. 363.

must stand for the spirit of faithlessness; but certainly it would be absurd to interpret the spirit of faithlessness as destroyed in the very early days of the Reformation, even prior to the destruction of the monasteries. I take it, rather, that the lion, Sansfoy, and Sansloy all represent actual men, and that the deaths of the lion and of Sansfoy refer to the actual physical deaths of some protector of the faith and of some one of its enemies.

The lion I believe to be Thomas Cromwell. In the eyes of the sixteenth-century Churchman, Cromwell figured as a spiritual leader and a martyr. This is the uniform interpretation given his character by all writers of the English Church. Subsequent centuries have, to be sure, discovered the real truth about the man, and we now think of him as the enemy of freedom, a minister self-trained in the school of Machiavelli.[1] But by the Churchmen of his own and the succeeding generation he was regarded as the stalwart champion of reform, the enemy of the papacy, the good friend of Cranmer, Ridley, and Latimer, their leader and fellow worker in establishing the Church upon a sound body of doctrine.

Foxe, who both expressed and molded the sentiment of Elizabethan Churchmen, credits Cromwell with the suppression of the abbeys and monasteries in the following language:

> Now somewhat would be said likewise of the noble Acts, the memorable Examples and worthy Vertues, not drowned by ease of Honour in him, but increased rather, and quickned by advancement of Authority and Place, to work more abundantly in the Commonwealth. Among the which his worthy Acts and other manifold

---

[1] Cf. the interesting study of his character in Van Dyke's Renaissance Portraits [New York, 1905], p. 138.

Vertues, in this one chiefly above all other riseth his commendation, for his singular Zeal and laborious Travel bestowed in restoring the true Church of Christ, and subverting the Synagogue of Antichrist, the Abbeys, I mean, and Religious houses of Friers and Monks. For so it pleased Almighty God, by the means of the said Lord Cromwel, to induce the King to suppress first the Chauntries, then the Friers Houses and small Monasteries, till at length all the Abbeys in England, both great and less, were utterly overthrown and pluckt up by the roots. . . . For my part I never saw yet in this Realm any such Cromwel since Cromwels time, whose heart and courage might not sooner have been subverted with the Mony and Bribes of Abbats, than he to have subverted any Abbey in all England.[1]

Then, after discussing at length the evil of the monasteries, he concludes :

All which things well considered, what marvel is it then, if God of his just judgment did set up the foresaid Cromwel to destroy these sinful houses, whom their own corruptions could suffer no longer to stand?[2]

Several explanations suggest themselves for the choice of the lion as the symbol of this grim minister. Reference may be had to the hardy origin of Cromwell as a smith's son ; or the savageness of the beast may be designed to suggest the brutal dispatch with which Cromwell executed his reform ; or, more likely yet, the lion is chosen because the beast figures both on the arms and on the crest of Cromwell, — a common method of identification in allegory.[3]

By the thirsty land drinking up the blood of Kirkrapine is meant the dissemination of the monastic wealth, which

[1] Actes and Monuments (ed. of 1684), Vol. II, p. 421.
[2] Ibid. p. 423. Cf. also Strype, Ecclesiastical Memorials (ed. of 1824), Vol. I, pt. 1, pp. 534, 561, et al.
[3] Cf. Doyle, Official Baronage of England, Vol. I, p. 690. Observe the similar way in which Surrey identifies himself in one of his poems (Padelford, Early Sixteenth Century Lyrics, p. 57).

Foxe justifies on the ground that only by this means could possible future restoration of the monasteries be forestalled.[1]

If the lion is Cromwell, who is Sansloy? I think we find the answer again in Foxe. After concluding the account of Cromwell's services in destroying the monasteries, Foxe elaborates upon his subsequent constructive work for the Church, a service allegorically set forth in the lion's attendance upon Una after the extinction of Kirkrapine. Then the account takes up the story of Cromwell's fall, introducing it with the following words:

> While the Lord Cromwel was thus blessedly occupied in profiting the common wealth, and purging the Church of Christ, it hapned to him, as commonly it doth to all good Men, that where any excellency of vertue appeareth, there envie creepeth in, and where true piety seeketh most after Christ, there some persecution followeth withal.
>
> This, I say, as he was labouring in the Commonwealth and doing good to the poor afflicted saints, helping them out of trouble, the malice of his Enemies so wrought, continually hunting for matter against him, that they never ceased, till in the end they by false trains and crafty surmises brought him out of the Kings Favour.
>
> The chief and principal Enemy against him was Stephen Gardiner, Bishop of Winchester; who ever disdaining and envying the State and Felicity of the Lord Cromwel, and now taking his occasion by the Marriage of Lady Anne of Cleve, being a stranger and forein, put in the Kings ears what a perfect thing it were to the quiet of the Realm, and establishment to the Kings succession, to have an English Queen and Prince that were meer English; so that in conclusion, the Kings affection, the more it was diminished from the late married Anne of Cleve, the less favour he bare unto Cromwel. Besides this Gardiner, there lacked not other Friends also, and ill willers in the Court about the King, which little made for Cromwel both for his Religion which they maligned, and for other private grudges also incident by the way.[2]

---
[1] Actes and Monuments, Vol. II, p. 423.
[2] Ibid. pp. 431–432.

Again, in introducing the injunctions against English books, sects, and sacramentaries, Foxe writes:

> As the Lord of his goodness had raised up Thomas Cromwel to be a Friend and Patron to the Gospel, so on the contrary side Satan (which is Adversary and Enemy to all good things) had his Organ also, which was Stephen Gardiner, by all wiles and subtil means to impeach and put back the same.[1]

In like vein Hall in his "Chronicle"[2] and Strype in his "Ecclesiastical Memorials"[3] attribute the overthrow of Cromwell to the antagonism of Gardiner, and it was clearly the prevailing belief of the sixteenth-century Churchmen that Cromwell and Gardiner were pitted against each other as the leaders respectively of the English Church party and of the Romanists, and that Cromwell's fall was due to his adversaries' cunning.[4] If then the lion symbolizes Cromwell, Sansloy symbolizes Gardiner. "Sansloy" was a very proper name for one who was credited with undermining the principles of true religion with all craft and subtlety, with being the chief instigator of Protestant persecutions, with deceiving the king by threats of foreign enemies and civil tumults, and even with plotting to murder Elizabeth, the heroine of the "Faerie Queene," as a child.[5]

Just as Una fell into the hands of Sansloy when the lion was slain, so, in the defeat of Cromwell, Gardiner gained control of the ecclesiastical policy, laid rude hands upon the Church, and tried to recover it for Romanism.

---

[1] Actes and Monuments, Vol. II, p. 369.
[2] P. 838.   [3] Vol. I, pt. 1, p. 561.
[4] Cf. the play, "The Life and Death of Thomas, Lord Cromwell" (Ancient British Drama, Vol. I, pp. 360–380), first printed in 1602, in which this struggle is presented in dramatic form. In this play the character of Cromwell is extravagantly idealized.
[5] D. N. B. Vol. VII, p. 864; Ecclesiastical Memorials, Vol. III, pt. 1, p. 131.

The Injunctions of 1539, — injunctions against English translations of the Bible, against discussion of the sacraments, and in support of holy bread and water and other rites, — the martyrdom of Lambert, and the famous Six Articles were the introductory steps in this activity. Foxe thus prefaces the summary of these "crafty fetches" of "this wily Winchester":

> To many which be yet alive, and can testifie these things, it is not unknown, how variable the state of Religion stood in these days; how hardly and with what difficulty it came forth, what chances and changes it suffered. Even as the King was ruled and gave ear sometime to one, sometime to another, so one while it went forward, at another season as much backward again, and sometime clean altered and changed for a season, according as they could prevail which were about the King. So long as Queen Anne lived, the Gospel had indifferent success.
>
> After that she, by sinister instigation of some about the King, was made away, the course of the Gospel began again to decline, but that the Lord then stirred up the Lord Cromwel, opportunely to help in that behalf. Who, no doubt, did much avail, for the increase of Gods true Religion, and much more had brought to perfection, if the pestilent Adversaries, maligning the prosperous glory of the Gospel, by contrary practising had not craftily undermined him and supplanted his vertuous proceedings. By the means of which Adversaries it came to pass after the taking away of the said Cromwel, that the state of Religion more and more decayed, during all the residue of the reign of King Henry.
>
> Among these Adversaries above mentioned, the chief Captain was Stephen Gardiner, Bishop of Winchester; who with his Confederates and Adherents, disdaining at the state of the Lord Cromwel, and at the late marriage of the Lady Anne of Cleve, . . . as also grieved partly at the dissolution of the Monasteries, and fearing the growing of the Gospel, sought all occasions how to interrupt these happy beginnings, and to train the King to their own purpose.[1]

[1] Actes and Monuments, Vol. II, p. 370.

Sansloy's misdirected attack upon the disguised Archimago is in general allusion, I should think, to Gardiner's unwitting assault upon the Roman Catholic Church in upholding the divorce proceedings of Henry; as soon as he appreciated that an actual change in religion was coming in the wake of the divorce, he swung around and launched an aggressive counter propaganda of Romanism.

If Sansloy is Gardiner, who is Sansfoy, the Saracen, attended by Duessa, who, in the story of the second canto, is vanquished and killed by the Red Cross Knight? The description of the character concludes:

> full large of limbe and every joint
> He was, and cared not for God or man a point.[1]

And when he rode against the Red Cross Knight, it is said that

> He, prickt with pride
> And hope to winne his Ladies heart that day,
> Forth spurred fast.[2]

Sansfoy must be some man high in the Church, of spiritual kinship with Gardiner, large of body and proud and disdainful of spirit, ambitious to make the Roman Catholic Church his mistress, who was struck down by Henry prior to the ascendancy of Cromwell and Gardiner. Only one character can possibly meet these requirements, — Cardinal Wolsey.

In the opinion of the Elizabethan Protestants, Gardiner was the successor of Wolsey as the leader of the Roman Catholics. Wolsey had indeed recommended him to the Pope in a well-known letter as "Primary Secretary of the most secret counsels" and as the very "half of himself:

[1] F. Q. I. 2. 12.   [2] Ibid. I. 2. 14.

than whom none was dearer to him."[1] Of the cardinal's pride, his greed, his falseness, and his inordinate ambition to secure the papal throne, what contemporary record is silent![2] Nor could a better pseudonym than "Sansfoy" have been chosen for this worldly cardinal, who expressed as completely as any of the De Medici the pagan spirit of the Renaissance. He was, indeed, England's one perfect exponent of that spirit, and his spiritual deficiency must have been strikingly evident to one who, like Spenser, never allowed his sympathy with classical traditions to threaten his faith.

As the Red Cross Knight became the associate and defender of the disguised Duessa upon the death of Sansfoy, so, upon the overthrow of Wolsey, Henry in turn began to play a false rôle in religion, and like Wolsey made the Church the mistress of his own vanity and selfishness. Hardly had Wolsey drawn his last breath, before the blasphemous vanity of Henry forced from a reluctant clergy the recognition of himself as Supreme Head of the Church, a title that he later forced Parliament itself to concede. In throwing off the papal yoke, Henry acted as the champion of reform, but he failed to take advantage of this initial service, and his influence soon became reactionary, so that by his attitude toward ecclesiastical reform he hindered the expression of truth through a purified Church, and by his immoral conduct violated the principles of truth as a rule of private life.

What is the historical counterpart of the "deceiving image" that resembles Una, but is not she, and that

---

[1] Ecclesiastical Memorials, Vol. I, pt. 1, p. 137.
[2] Cf. Hall, Chronicle, pp. 759, 773, 774; Actes and Monuments, Vol. II, pp. 197-209.

appears to the Red Cross Knight in the embrace of a lusty young squire? I suggest that this image may stand for Lutheranism, against which, in 1529, the year prior to the death of Wolsey, Henry issued "a proclamation for resisting and withstanding of most damnable heresies, sown within this realm by the disciples of Luther, and other heretics, perverters of Christ's religion";[1] and that the squire may stand for Germany. Una was veiled, the knight had never beheld her face, and he was therefore easily deceived into mistaking the image for his lady; so the truth, as embodied in the doctrines of the English Church, was not yet revealed, and Henry could not discriminate between the system of Luther and the true faith. The spectacle of Lutheranism disgusted him, and in turning away from it he turned away from the true reform which was to follow, and of which it was only a semblance. This interpretation, making Lutheranism a product of Rome and only an imitation of true religion, is probably in line with Spenser's own attitude towards Lutherans, for the feeling against Lutheranism was very pronounced among the Low Churchmen of Spenser's day; they were followers of Zwingli, and classed the Lutherans with Papists. Writing to Rudolph Gualter, in 1576, Bishop Horn declared Lutheranism "a great disturber of Christianity,"[2] and William Turner, Dean of Wells, classed Lutherans with wolves, Papists, Sadducees, and Herodians. Archbishop Grindal, the mentor of Spenser, in common with all those leaders who had come under the influence of the Swiss schools, was a pronounced antagonist of the

---

[1] Cf. Actes and Monuments, Vol. II, pp. 236 ff., for the proclamation entire.
[2] Zurich Letters, Vol. I, p. 321.

Lutherans. In a letter written to Henry Bullinger of Zurich in 1566, after speaking of the entire agreement between the doctrines of the English clergy and the Swiss, as expressed in the Helvetic Confession, he proceeds to defend the wisdom of the Low-Church party in acquiescing in the desires of Elizabeth and Parliament with reference to ecclesiastical garments, and concludes:

and we do not regret our resolution; for in the meantime, the Lord giving the increase, our churches are enlarged and established, which under other circumstances would have become a prey to the Ecebolians, Lutherans, and semi-papists.[1]

If the dwarf has any special historical significance, I have failed to discover it. Perhaps some other student may be able to interpret this interesting character.

Cantos IV and V renew the story of the Red Cross Knight. Led by Duessa, he now visits the house of Pride. There Lucifera, the queen of Pride, is seated upon her throne, surrounded by an obsequious court. The usher, "Vanitie by name," conducts the knight to the lowest stair, where he makes obeisance to the disdainful queen, who barely notices him. The company, however, are glad to welcome him, and Duessa moves among them as an old-time favorite. Suddenly the queen rises, and, seating herself in a coach drawn by six beasts on which ride her counselors, the other deadly sins, rides out for a pleasure trip. As the knight is returning from this excursion, he is confronted by Sansjoy; whereupon they fall to angry words over the shield of Sansfoy, which the dwarf bears upside down in derision. Thereupon a battle is arranged for the next day. That night the fickle

[1] Zurich Letters, Vol. I, p. 169; cf. also Vol. I, p. 177; Vol. II, pp. 143, 241, 245; Vol. III, p. 682.

Duessa seeks out the couch of Sansjoy, to wish him well in the conflict of the morrow.

Morning come, all repair to the lists, eager for the duel. Fortune favors now one, now the other. At length Sansjoy strikes the Red Cross Knight a blow that makes him reel, and Duessa, thinking the end has come, shouts to Sansjoy, "Thine the shield, and I, and all." But the knight, hearing these shameful words, revives, and with exceeding fury raises his sword for a deadly blow; but unseen powers are against him, for Duessa, unsuspected, throws a magic cloud about the false Sansjoy. All think that he has been borne away to the lower world, and the Red Cross Knight is proclaimed victor. That night Duessa secures the aid of Night, an ancestor of Sansjoy, to bear the wounded man to the realm of Pluto, that Æsculapius may heal his wounds. Duessa herself rides in the chariot of Night amid grisly sights. Thence she returns to the palace in search of the knight, only to find him gone. He and his prudent dwarf had fled, warned by a glimpse of the dungeons beneath.

The description of the household of Pride is the first of those "purple patches" which are to be met with throughout the course of the poem. Thereby is set forth that lust of the flesh, and that lust of the eyes, and that pride of life which gave such a grievous turn to the career of the king. In his surrender to the things that are in the world, Henry violated the sanctity of religion by assuming the headship of the Church, and the sanctity of social morals by letting loose the tempest of his passions. The application of the allegory is to be regarded as general rather than specific.

But what is to be made of Sansjoy, the sorrowful one, who is so mysteriously snatched away and borne to the distant realm of Pluto? If Sansfoy and Sansloy are actual historical characters, assuredly Sansjoy should be so as well. I have no convincing suggestion to make. May Sansjoy be Cardinal Pole, who, with falling tears, besought Henry not to yield to his sinful lust for Anne Boleyn, — who directed against the king his great tractate "*Pro Ecclesiasticae Unitatis Defensione*" in support of the papal supremacy, and who was snatched from the wrath of Henry by the summons of Rome? "Sansjoy" would be a very proper appellation for this austere Papist, who had beheld his very mother a sacrifice to the wrath of Henry.

In Canto VI Una is delivered from Sansloy by a band of satyrs,

> A rude, mishapen, monstrous rablement,

whose appearance the evil knight "durst not byde." Una soon puts away her fears of them when the kind-hearted beings "kisse her feete, and fawne on her with count'-nance fayne," and she walks forth surrounded by a shouting and singing throng who strew the ground with branches and worship her as queen. With them she remains for a season as their teacher.

At length it fortunes that a warlike knight, Sir Satyrane, born among the satyrs, as is his custom after labors abroad, returns to visit his native folk.

> He had in armes abroad wonne muchell fame,
> And fild far landes with glorie of his might;
> Plaine, faithfull, true, and enimy of shame,
> And ever lov'd to fight for Ladies right.

As a lad he had been trained in courage by a sturdy father:

> For all he taught the tender ymp was but
> To banish cowardize and bastard feare:
> His trembling hand he would him force to put
> Upon the Lyon and the rugged Beare;

And from the she Beares teats her whelps to teare;
And eke wyld roring Buls he would him make
To tame, and ryde their backes, not made to beare;
And the Robuckes in flight to overtake,
That everie beast for feare of him did fly, and quake.

Grown to young manhood, he had

Desyrd of forreine foemen to be knowne,
And far abroad for straunge adventures sought;
In which his might was never overthrowne;
But through al Faery lond his famous worth was blown.

This knight submits himself to the tutelage of Una, and then offers to conduct her out of the forest. On the way thence they are met by Archimago, again disguised, who pretends that the Red Cross Knight has been slain by a Saracen, just now hard by. The eager Sir Satyrane hastens to seek the Saracen, while Una slowly follows. The Saracen, really Sansloy, and Sir Satyrane at once engage, and are both bathed in blood when Una arrives. Seeing his erstwhile victim again, the lust of Sansloy revives, but he is intercepted by Sir Satyrane, who forces him once more to the combat. Thereupon Una, afraid lest she again fall into the power of the evil Sansloy, seeks safety in flight.

If the interpretation of the political allegory of the preceding cantos has been in the main correct, and if the allegory follows the sequence of history without prolonged hiatus, Sir Satyrane must represent a man who became the recognized champion of the reform movement at the death of Cromwell. Moreover, to be consistent with the character of Sir Satyrane, he must be a man sprung from the people, — for of course the episode of the satyrs means that the spirit of true religion was fostered and harbored by the common folk when its integrity was threatened in high places,—

a man plain, honest, and faithful, a man of physical prowess, and one who had earned distinction in foreign courts.

According to Foxe, the man who assumed the reform leadership on Cromwell's death and upon whom fell at the death of the viceroy the mantle of Gardiner's hate was Cranmer:

> For after the apprehension of the Lord Cromwel, when the Adversaries of the Gospel thought all things sure now on their side, it was so appointed amongst them, that ten or twelve Bishops, and other learned Men, joyned together in Commission, came to the said Archbishop of Canterbury for the establishing of certain Articles of our Religion, which the Papists then thought to win to their purpose against the said Archbishop. For having now the Lord Cromwel fast and sure, they thought all had been safe, and sure for ever: as indeed to all Mens reasonable consideration, that time appeared so dangerous, that there was no manner of hope that Religion reformed should any one week longer stand, such account was then made of the Kings untowardness thereunto. Insomuch, that of all those Commissioners there was not one left to stay on the Archbishops part, but he alone against them all stood in the defence of the truth.[1]

Then follows the account of Cranmer's victory in this contention, through the king's favor, though "many wagers would have been laid in London, that he should have been laid up with Cromwel at that time in the Tower for his stiff standing to his tackle." This account is succeeded by the well-known and picturesque story of Cranmer's summons before the council and his dramatic producing of the king's ring. The story, which is introduced as follows, shows the enmity of Gardiner:

> Notwithstanding, not long after that, certain of the Council, whose names need not to be repeated, by the inticement and provocation of his ancient enemy the Bishop of Winchester, and other of the same

[1] Actes and Monuments, Vol. III, p. 538.

sect, attempted the King against him, declaring plainly, that the Realm was so infected with Heresies and Hereticks, that it was dangerous for his Highness farther to permit it unreformed, lest peradventure by long suffering, such contention should arise, and ensue in the Realm among his Subjects, that thereby might spring horrible commotions, and uproars, like as in some parts of Germany it did not long ago. The enormity whereof they could not impute to any so much, as to the Archbishop of Canterbury, who by his own Preaching, and his Chaplains, had filled the whole Realm full of divers pernicious Heresies.

To this episode succeeds the account of the "popish conspiracy" in Kent, which was found to be instigated by the letters of Gardiner.[1]

As Foxe makes it so very clear that Cranmer succeeded Cromwell as the leader of the reform party, and that the Bishop of Winchester was the aggressive and malicious leader of the opponents, the presumption strongly favors assigning the character of Sir Satyrane to Cranmer.

Moreover, it could properly be said of Cranmer,

> He had in armes abroad wonne muchell fame,
> And fild far landes with glorie of his might,

for he had been sent abroad in connection with the king's divorce, had boldly declared the English contention to the Pope, had waited in vain for an adversary qualified to dispute with him, and had thence alone sought the court of the emperor and won the assent of his council.

Again, it is interesting to observe that whereas Spenser describes Sir Satyrane as

> Plaine, faithfull, true, and enimy of shame,

Foxe devotes several pages to showing how fully Cranmer measured up to all of the desiderata of a bishop,

---

[1] Actes and Monuments, Vol. III, p. 540.

concluding with the following sentences, which point out the archbishop's faithful devotion to truth:

> Neither shall he deserve the name of a Bishop, if either for dread or meed, affection or favour, he do at any time or in any point swerve from the truth. As in this behalf the worthy constancy of this said Archbishop never, for the most part shrunk for any manner of storm; but was so many ways tried, that neither favour of his Prince, nor fear of the indignation of the same, nor any other worldly respect could alienate or change his purpose, grounded upon that infallible Doctrine of the Gospel.[1]

Like Sir Satyrane, Cranmer was much given to physical activities, and the suggestion for the prowess of Sir Satyrane and for adapting the account of Atlantê's training of Rogero to his youthful education [2] may have been prompted by Cranmer's well-known fondness for sports and the careful training in athletics that he received from his father. On the authority of an early manuscript life of Cranmer, Strype writes:

> Though his father were minded to have his son educated in learning, yet he would not he should be ignorant of civil and gentlemanlike exercises: insomuch that he used himself to shoot. And many times his father permitted him to hunt and hawk, and to ride rough horses: so that when he was bishop, he feared not to ride the roughest horses that came into his stables; which he would do very comely. As otherwise at all times there was not any in his house that would become an horse better. And after his studies, when it was time for recreation, he would both hawk and hunt, the game being prepared for him. And sometimes he would shoot in the long-bow, and many times kill the deer with his cross-bow, though his sight was not perfect; for he was poreblind.[3]

The highly colored recital of Sir Satyrane's prowess and exploits is amply justified by the exigencies of the allegory.

---

[1] Actes and Monuments, Vol. III, p. 538.　[2] Orlando Furioso, 7. 5. 7.
[3] Memorials of Archbishop Cranmer, Vol. I, p. 2.

Like the hero of the canto, Cranmer was a man of the people, and they understood him and regarded him with admiration and affection.[1]

But if Cranmer is to be identified with Sir Satyrane, what explanation is to be offered of Sir Satyrane's illegitimate birth? I confess that I have no explanation to offer, other than to suggest that this conception is purely gratuitous, and introduced merely because in line with the satyr tradition.

I do not feel altogether satisfied that I have solved the identity of this odd character, but I present my suggestion for what it is worth. If the suggestion be proved incorrect, it may at least prevent some other student from following a wrong trail.[2]

---

[1] Actes and Monuments, Vol. III, pp. 534-537; Arber, An English Garner (ed. 1895), Vol. IV, p. 160.

[2] For a time I thought that this character was meant to portray Hugh Latimer, the most popular preacher of the epoch and the most fearless, a man to whom his contemporaries affectionately alluded as "a doughty old soldier" (cf. Works of Bishop Ridley, p. 146 [Parker Society]). Latimer was sprung from the people, he was their idol, and he preferred to live and work among them, more or less remote from the centers. While the account of the youthful training of Sir Satyrane is adapted from the education of Rogero, I had thought that Spenser might have taken his hint from Latimer's account of his own training as contained in one of his sermons: "My father was delighted to teach me to shoot with the bow. He taught me how to draw, how to lay my body to the bow, not to draw with strength of arm as other nations do, but with the strength of the body." As a student at Cambridge Latimer first demonstrated his masculine strength in debate, and from that time until his death, save when forcibly silenced, he was fighting the battles of reform, and in all the notable disputes in which he figured, as the poet truthfully says, "his might was never overthrowne."

From 1531 to 1535 Latimer was rector at West Kineton in Wiltshire, on the border of Gloucestershire, and from 1535 to 1539 he was Bishop of Winchester. As a result of these nine years of labor in the West counties, the reform movement there had a very sturdy growth. Latimer was often drawn to London, now to defend his doctrines before bishops, now to preach before the king, but he was always impatient to

Cantos VII–VIII and the opening stanzas of Canto IX narrate the capture of the Red Cross Knight by the giant Orgoglio and the deliverance wrought by Prince Arthur.

When Duessa returns to the castle of Pride and finds the knight gone, she starts in search of him. Ere long she finds him, weary, seated by a fountain, his armor laid aside. Once more she insinuates herself into his good will, and they surrender themselves to enjoyment of the pleasant shade which shields them against the boiling sun, and of the sweet music of the birds. The fountain bubbles freshly at their feet and the knight, ignorant of its source and effect, drinks of the water. Straightway his strength is gone, for the presiding nymph was one who had, from weariness, deserted the chase of Diana, and against whom the goddess had decreed that her waters should wax dull

---

be back among his own people; once he complains bitterly that he is detained from them at Eastertide.

Latimer towers above all his contemporaries as the enemy of lawlessness. In season and out of season he was preaching virtue and righteousness in public and private life, reproving the king, the bishops, and the clergy at large for their worldliness, with absolutely no respect for persons. The man who dared to send to the king as a New Year's present a napkin embroidered with the words "*Fornicatores et adulteros judicabit Dominus,*" might quite properly be chosen to figure in an allegory of the English Reformation as the arch-opponent of lawlessness. Certainly it would have been acceptable to Elizabeth thus to identify the sturdy martyr, who, in his last imprisonment under Mary, prayed without ceasing that "God would preserve the Lady Elizabeth, and make her a comfort to this comfortless realm of England."

And yet this interpretation interferes with a chronological sequence to the allegory, for it was not after the death of Cromwell, but before, that Latimer came into prominence as the opponent of lawlessness, and of Gardiner as its exponent. In 1539, the year of Cromwell's death, he resigned his bishopric because of the Six Articles, and was then silenced for several years.

Moreover, if the statement that Sir Satyrane had won much military fame *abroad* is to be taken literally, Latimer is excluded, for he was never out of England.

and slow, and that all who drank thereof should be enfeebled. Yet, "careless of his health and of his fame," the knight still courts his false lady,

> Pourd out in loosenesse on the grassy grownd.

Foolish knight! for straightway with a "dreadfull sownd" a giant, "horrible and hye," bursts upon them. It is Orgoglio, child of "blustring Eolus" and Earth, who brought him forth

> Puft up with emptie wynd, and fild with sinfull cryme.

"Disarmd, disgrast, and inwardly dismayde," the knight feebly rises to defend himself, but though he succeeds in dodging the blow of the giant's mace, he is stunned by the vibration. Thereupon the giant is about to kill him, when Duessa cries to him to make the knight a bondslave, and to take her for a paramour. The giant willingly agrees, takes Duessa into his arms, and thrusts the knight into a dungeon.

> From that day forth Duessa was his deare,
> And highly honourd in his haughtie eye:
> He gave her gold and purple pall to weare,
> And triple crowne set on her head full hye,
> And her endowd with royall majestye.
> Then, for to make her dreaded more of men,
> And peoples hartes with awfull terror tye,
> A monstrous beast ybredd in filthy fen
> He chose, which he had kept long time in darksom den.
> . . . .
>
> His tayle was stretched out in wondrous length,
> That to the hous of hevenly gods it raught:
> And with extorted powre, and borrow'd strength,
> The everburning lamps from thence it braught,
> And prowdly threw to ground, as things of naught;

And underneath his filthy feet did tread
The sacred thinges, and holy heastes foretaught.
Upon this dreadfull Beast with sevenfold head
He sett the false Duessa, for more aw and dread.

Seeing his master thus captive, the dwarf picks up his idle armor and departs in great distress. Ere long he meets Una, and imparts the news to her. She is prostrated with grief, but comfort comes in the person of Prince Arthur, an errant knight with goodly squire, who promises his aid. The resplendent armor of this knight surpasses all else on earth. In the midst of his breastplate is a precious stone, shaped like a lady's head; but most dazzling is his marvelous shield:

His warlike shield all closely cover'd was,
Ne might of mortall eye be ever seene;
Not made of steele, nor of enduring bras,
Such earthly mettals soon consumed beene,
But all of Diamond perfect pure and cleene
It framed was, one massy entire mould,
Hewen out of Adamant rocke with engines keene,
That point of speare it never percen could,
Ne dint of direfull sword divide the substance would.

The same to wight he never wont disclose,
But whenas monsters huge he would dismay,
Or daunt unequall armies of his foes,
Or when the flying heavens he would affray;
For so exceeding shone his glistring ray,
That Phœbus golden face it did attaint,
As when a cloud his beames doth over-lay;
And silver Cynthia wexed pale and faynt,
As when her face is staynd with magicke arts constraint.

No magicke arts hereof had any might,
Nor bloody wordes of bold Enchaunters call;

But all that was not such as seemd in sight
Before that shield did fade, and suddeine fall:
And when him list the raskall routes appall,
Men into stones therewith he could transmew,
And stones to dust, and dust to nought at all;
And, when him list the prouder lookes subdew,
He would them gazing blind, or turne to other hew.

Guided by the dwarf, they come to the castle. Beneath its walls the squire blows his "horne of bugle small."

Wyde wonders over all
Of that same hornes great virtues weren told,
Which had approved bene in uses manifold.

Was never wight that heard that shrilling sownd,
But trembling feare did feel in every vaine:
Three miles it might be easy heard arownd,
And Ecchoes three aunswer'd it selfe againe:
No false enchauntment, nor deceiptfull traine,
Might once abide the terror of that blast,
But presently was void and wholly vaine:
No gate so strong, no locke so firme and fast,
But with that percing noise flew open quite, or brast.

Forth rushes Orgoglio, followed by Duessa mounted upon her beast, whose mouths are bloody "with late cruell feast," and the battle is on. The giant raises his fearful mace, but the agile knight skillfully avoids the blow, and then when the giant struggles to free his club, deep buried in the ground, smites off his great left arm.

That when his deare Duessa heard, and saw
The evil stownd that daungerd her estate,
Unto his aide she hastily did draw
Her dreadfull beast: who, swolne with blood of late,
Came ramping forth with proud presumpteous gate,

And threatned all his heades like flaming brandes.
But him the Squire made quickly to retrate,
Encountring fiers with single sword in hand ;
And twixt him and his Lord did like a bulwarke stand.

The proud Duessa, full of wrathfull spight,
And fiers disdaine to be affronted so,
Enforst her purple beast with all her might,
That stop out of the way to overthroe,
Scorning the let of so unequall foe :
But nathemore would that corageous swayne
To her yeeld passage gainst his Lord to goe,
But with outrageous strokes did him restraine,
And with his body bard the way atwixt them twaine.

Then tooke the angrie witch her golden cup,
Which still she bore, replete with magick artes ;
Death and despeyre did many thereof sup,
And secret poyson through their inner partes,
Th' eternall bale of heavie wounded harts ;
Which, after charmes and some enchauntments said,
She lightly sprinkled on his weaker partes :
Therewith his sturdie corage soon was quayd,
And all his sences were with suddein dread dismayd.

So downe he fell before the cruell beast,
Who on his neck his bloody clawes did seize,
That life nigh crusht out of his panting brest :
No powre he had to stirre, nor will to rize.
That when the carefull knight gan well avise,
He lightly left the foe with whom he fought,
And to the beast gan turne his enterprise ;
For wondrous anguish in his hart it wrought,
To see his loved Squyre into such thraldom brought :

And, high advauncing his blood-thirstie blade,
Stroke one of those deformed heades so sore,
That of his puissaunce proud ensample made :
His monstrous scalpe downe to his teeth it tore,
And that misformed shape misshaped more.

Enraged at this mishap, Orgoglio strikes Prince Arth upon the shield and doubles him to the ground. But it is his last assault, for the knight regains his feet, and with his sparkling blade smites off the right leg of his adversary, and

> The knight, then lightly leaping to the pray,
> With mortall steele him smot againe so sore,
> That headlesse his unweldy bodie lay,
> All wallowd in his owne fowle bloody gore,
> Which flowed from his wounds in wondrous store.
> But, soone as breath out of his brest did pas,
> That huge great body, which the Gyaunt bore,
> Was vanisht quite; and of that monstrous mas
> Was nothing left, but like an emptie blader was.
>
> Whose grievous fall when false Duessa spyde,
> Her golden cup she cast unto the ground,
> And crowned mitre rudely threw asyde:
> Such percing griefe her stubborne hart did wound,
> That she could not endure that dolefull stound
> But leaving all behind her fled away:
> The light-foot Squyre her quickly turnd around,
> And, by hard meanes enforcing her to stay,
> So brought unto his Lord as his deserved pray.

Then Prince Arthur enters the castle, which is found to be adorned with gold and costly hangings, though the floors are all vile "with blood of guiltlesse babes and innocents trew." The Red Cross Knight, half starved, is found and freed, and Duessa, stripped of her royal robes and purple pall, is allowed to "goe at will, and wander wayes unknowne."

After rest and refreshment, Prince Arthur tells of his mysterious origin, and of the vision of a lovely maid, whom he has come to "Faery land" to seek. Then there is an exchange of presents:

> Prince Arthur gave a boxe of Diamond sure,
> Embowd with gold and gorgeous ornament,

> Wherein were closd few drops of liquor pure,
> Of wondrous worth, and vertue excellent,
> That any wownd could heale incontinent.
> Which to requite, the Redcrosse knight him gave
> A booke, wherein his Saveours testament
> Was writt with golden letters rich and brave:
> A worke of wondrous grace, and hable soules to save.
>
> Thus beene they parted; Arthur on his way
> To seeke his love, and th' other for to fight
> With Unaes foe, that all her realme did pray.

I have been forced thus to go into detail in the story of these cantos because of the elaborate character of the allegory. The opening episode means, I take it, that Henry, weakened by that ungodly pride which led him to arrogate to himself the title of "Supreme Head of the Church," fell an easy victim to the temptations of the flesh. The wood stands, as ever, for the world, the songs of birds for its innocent pleasures, — perhaps the woodland pageants of which Henry was so fond, — and the waters of the fountain, for moral slothfulness and insensibility. The knight's amours with Duessa symbolize Henry's sensuality, that dulled and enervated his spiritual perception and unfitted him to see or to defend the truth. "Both carelesse of his health and of his fame" is a true summary of the conduct of his later years.

In this introductory scene with the knight, Duessa, or Falsehood, is seen in her aspect as false living, — that immorality that overtakes the man who has separated himself from spiritual truth. In her connivance with Orgoglio Duessa typifies, on the other hand, false belief, and as false belief she stands of course for the Roman Catholic doctrine and practice. The imagery with which she is depicted is borrowed from the description of the woman of the Apocalypse, the mother of harlots and abominations of the earth.[1] In the Revelation the woman is interpreted as "that great city, which reigneth over the Kings of the earth," meaning Rome ; and as the reform writers constantly referred to this woman and invariably identified her with spiritual Rome, Spenser found this feature of his allegory ready to hand.[2] Like the harlot of the Apocalypse,[3] Duessa is arrayed in purple and gold, thus symbolizing the gorgeous ecclesiastical garments and the rich deckings of the Church of Rome, as well as her bloodguiltiness. In his elaborate exposition of the Apocalypse,[4] Bishop Bale thus vituperatively interprets these deckings of "the holy mother, the madam of mischief and proud synagogue of Satan" :

> In token that this hypocritical church standeth in the murder of innocents, this woman is here gorgeously apparelled in purple, as guilty of their deaths which hath been slain, and also in fresh scarlet, as evermore fresh and ready to continue in the same bloodshedding. For if such terrible slaughter were not, the true christian faith should increase, to the great diminishment of her glory.
> She is in like case flourishingly decked with gold, precious stone, and pearls, not only in her manifold kinds of ornaments, as in her copes, corporasses, chasubles, tunicles, stoles, fannoms, and mitres, but also in mystery of counterfeit godliness. Many outward brags maketh this painted church of Christ, of his gospel, and of his apostles, signified by the gold, precious stone, and pearls ; which is but a glittering colour : for nothing mindeth she less than to follow them in conversation of living.[5]

[1] Rev. xvii.
[2] Cf. Select Works of Bishop Bale, pp. 426, 493, 496–498 ; Works of Bishop Ridley, pp. 53–55, 415 ; Hooper, Later Writings, p. 554 ; Works of Archbishop Cranmer, Vol. II, p. 63 ; etc., all in the publications of the Parker Society.   [3] Rev. xvii, 4.
[4] "The Image of Both Churches," Select Works of Bishop Bale, pp. 249–640.   [5] P. 497

The seven-headed beast is adapted from the Apocalyptic beast of the sea,[1] with certain characteristics borrowed from the Apocalyptic dragon.[2] For the woman, the beast, and the dragon of St. John, Spenser has substituted the woman, the beast, and Orgoglio. The reason for this is apparent, for, with a good eye to a climax, the poet wished to reserve the dragon for the supreme and concluding struggle of the book. As the whore symbolizes Rome, so the beast is invariably interpreted as Antichrist, the bestial body of Satan.[3] Sometimes the beast is thus identified with the Pope, as the peculiar embodiment of the spirit of Antichrist,[4] but more often with the whole company of Papists as "one universal Antichrist":[5]

> This beast is the great Antichrist that was spoken of afore, or the beastly body of the devil, comprehending in him popes, patriarchs, cardinals, legates, bishops, doctors. abbots, priors, priests, and pardoners, monks, canons, friars, nuns, and so forth; temporal governors also, as emperors, kings, princes, dukes, earls, lords, justices, deputies, judges, lawyers, mayors, bailiffs, constables, and so forth.[6]

The seven heads of the beast are variously interpreted: sometimes, for example, as Antichrist's presumptuous doings for the seven ages of the Church; sometimes as the seven principal geographical divisions of the world; sometimes as the countries or kingdoms in which Roman Catholicism holds sway. It is in this latter sense that Spenser employs them, I believe; for the wounding of one of the heads of the beast and its subsequent healing was popularly applied to the emancipation of a country from

---

[1] Rev. xiii and xvii.   [2] Rev. xii.
[3] Cf. Works of Bishop Ridley, pp. 53, 415–418; Select Works of Bishop Bale, p. 424, etc.
[4] Cf. Ridley, p. 263.   [5] Bale, p. 426.   [6] Ibid. p. 496.

papal jurisdiction and practices and its subsequent return to them. Bale thus expressed this popular conception :

> Are not now in many parts of Germany, and in England also, the pope's pardons laid aside ; his power put down, his name abolished, his purgatory, pilgrimages, and other peltries utterly exiled; and so like to be within short space in other regions also? If this be not a deadly wounding of one of the beast's heads, I think there is none. . . . But the healing again of this mortal wound is like to mar all, and make the last error worse than the first. . . . Still remaineth their foul masses, etc.[1]

In describing the beast as bred in filthiness and for a long time kept in darkness, allusion is of course made to the superstition of the Middle Ages. The description of the tail of the beast — able to reach to the house of the heavenly gods and, with extorted power and borrowed strength, to take the ever-burning lamps and throw them to the ground — is adapted from the description of the Apocalyptic dragon, whose "tail drew the third part of the stars of heaven, and did cast them to the earth."[2] St. John therein alludes to Satan's successful tempting of certain of the angels, and Spenser probably had in mind those men who should have been illustrious in the Church, but whom Rome robbed of their heritage by her false teachings and made children of darkness. Such is the application given to the passage by Bale[3] and Sandys.[4]

[1] Bale, pp. 426-427.   [2] Rev. xii, 4.
[3] "And his tail drew towards him the third part of the stars, and in conclusion threw them down to the earth. By worldly promotions, lucre, favour, and other flattering fantasies, hath he tangled many learned men, and plucked them clean from Christ's true church and from the life of the gospel, so provoking them wholly to give themselves to the study of erroneous doctrine and lying prophecies, to seduce the worldly multitude, and keep them in perpetual blindness."
[4] Sermons, pp. 361-362 [Parker Society].

As Duessa represents the doctrine and worldly practices of Rome, and the beast — the universal Antichrist — the countries and people who were under the domination of Rome, so Orgoglio represents, I take it, the power of Rome that, save for the brief years of Edward's reign, had the upper hand in England from the passage of the Six Articles in 1539 to the Acts of Uniformity and Supremacy under Elizabeth in 1559. Henry had, to be sure, thrown off the yoke of Rome, but during the later years of his life the Church became increasingly Roman Catholic, and the cause of the national Church steadily lost ground. The conflict with Orgoglio is the allegorical story of the struggle against Roman Catholicism during this period. The ancestry of Orgoglio typifies its terrestrial and uninspired origin. True religion is derived from, and vitalized by, the Holy Spirit of God, but Roman Catholicism breathes only "emptie wind," and its parentage, which puffs it up with "arrogant delight," is pagan, — blustering and boastful emptiness, typified by Æolus. Quite consistently, therefore, when Arthur finally slays Orgoglio, only an empty bladder remains.

In his letter to Raleigh, Spenser identifies the character of Prince Arthur with "Magnificence," or great deeds. I take it that Spenser is here not thinking of any individual. In its severely political aspect the character stands for the national spirit of England, which expresses itself in the great things that it achieves, which, like the hero of this canto, had its origin enveloped in mystery, and which in legend finds its ideal exponent in King Arthur. It was this spirit that demanded the Magna Charta, that wrote "Piers Plowman," that won Crécy, Poitiers, and Agincourt, that inspired the Lollards, that silently revolted at the carnage of Mary, that hailed the accession of Elizabeth with a burst of enthusiastic joy, and that made the England of Elizabeth foremost among the nations. With something of flattery, but with commendable pride and patriotism as well, Spenser represents this spirit as seeking in England for the counterpart of its vision of a maid of transcendent charm; for Elizabeth's reign actually represented the ideal for which the England of "great deeds" had been striving.

In its spiritual aspect, the character symbolizes heavenly grace, for the opening stanza of Canto VIII introduces the narrative of the liberation of the Red Cross Knight by Prince Arthur and Una as follows:

> Ay me! how many perils doe enfold
> The righteous man, to make him daily fall,
> Were not that *heavenly grace* doth him uphold,
> And stedfast *truth* acquite him out of all.

Here Prince Arthur is identified with heavenly grace, as Una with truth. Heavenly grace and the national spirit are thus, as it were, fused together, for Spenser believed that God was thus using England to reveal the character of true religion; and when Prince Arthur does battle with Orgoglio, Christ and Antichrist, as it were, strive for the possession of England. The shield of Arthur, that outshines the beauty of the sun, that brings all things hidden to the light, — what else can it be than superlative Christian faith?

The diamond box, inclosing the drops of pure liquor able to heal any wound, which Prince Arthur gives to St. George in parting, I take to be the wine of the Communion service, which, through heavenly grace, was given to the English Church; and the book which the Red Cross Knight gives in return, the Book of Common

Prayer, the gift of the English Church, in which the testament of Christ, the holy sacrament, is "writ with golden letters rich and brave," — "a worke of wondrous grace, and hable soules to save." In this exchange is literal reference, I think, to the permanent establishment of Communion in two kinds and the final adoption of the Book of Common Prayer in 1559.

The squire, "the admirer of his [Arthur's] might," I take to be, as generally agreed, the body of reform clergy, and the horn to be the Bible, against which the false teachings and practices of the Roman Catholic Church cannot stand.

In the struggle between Prince Arthur and Orgoglio, the first telling blow is when the knight cuts off the left arm of the giant. Now it is the left arm which bears the shield, and the shield always typifies faith; and as the Mass was that which upheld the Roman Catholic faith, the cutting off of the arm would seem to typify the suppression of the Mass under Edward and the substitution of the Communion service. This would identify the episode with the early reign of Edward. As the dallying of the Red Cross Knight with Duessa rather clearly records the attitude of Henry's later years, this interpretation would be chronologically consistent.

Passing over the second episode for the moment, in the third episode Duessa sprinkles the liquor from her magic cup upon the squire and thus robs him of his strength. This cup is suggested by the "cup full of abominations"[1] which the harlot of the Apocalypse holds in her hand. The writers of the English Church were a unit in their interpretation of the meaning of this cup of abominations.

[1] Rev. xvii, 4.

In his "A Piteous Lamentation of the Miserable Estate of the Churche of Christ in Englande, in the Time of Queene May," Ridley thus explains it:

> By the abominations thereof, I understand all the whole trade of the Romish religion, under the name and title of Christ, which is contrary to the only rule of all true religion, that is, God's word. . . . But you would know, which be those merchandise, which I said this whore setteth forth to sell. . . . Surely, surely, they be not only all these abominations which are come into the church of England already (whereof I have spoken somewhat before) but also an innumerable rabblement of abominations and wicked abuses, which now must needs follow: as Popish pardons, pilgrimages, Romish purgatory, Romish masses, *placebo et dirige*, with trentals, and *scala coeli*, dispensations and immunities from all godly discipline, laws, and good order, pluralities, unions *tot quots*, with a thousand more.[1]

As the reform writers especially applied this cup of abominations to Mary's restoration of the Mass and the whole Roman Catholic régime, there can be small question that the magic cup of Duessa, potent for death and despair, antithetical to the diamond box of life-giving liquor, stands for the Mass and its deadening influence when forced by Mary upon the Church. The beast crushing the life out of the squire would then mean Mary's effort to wipe out Protestantism.

The second episode is the charge of the beast goaded on by Duessa, and its summary retreat before the sword of the stalwart squire. The political analogue must be the vigorous and effective opposition which the reform party offered the Roman Catholics in the days of Edward, as illustrated by the suppression of the insurrection in the West in 1549, and the radical teaching of such men as Ridley and Latimer. The blood dripping from the mouths

[1] Works, pp. 53–55; cf. also p. 415, and Bale, p. 497.

of the beast refers to the Protestant martyrdoms, and in the beast threatening "all his heads" is reference to the general opposition of Roman Catholics throughout Europe.

In the fourth episode Prince Arthur runs to the rescue of the squire and cleaves one of the heads of the beast to the teeth.[1] This I interpret as the divine intervention whereby Mary died and the Catholic Church lost England. When the Protestant movement seemed almost extinguished, heavenly grace intervened through the death of Mary. Elizabeth sitting under an oak in Hatfield Park, on hearing the news of Mary's death, exclaimed, "This is the Lord's doing; and it is marvelous in our eyes." Such was the voice of England.

The renewed effort of Orgoglio represents, I take it, the vigorous opposition to change which the Roman Catholics made at the beginning of Elizabeth's reign. This chapter of history is too familiar to need elaboration. So intense was the opposition that the convocation refused to hear of any change in the service; but Elizabeth, through Parliament, quickly retaliated, and first by the Act of Uniformity and then by the Act of Supremacy overpowered the Catholic spirit. The first of these acts may figure in the allegory as the cutting off of the right leg of the giant, the second as his decapitation. By this last act Elizabeth was acknowledged to be the supreme governor of the realm "as well in all spiritual or ecclesiastical things as temporal." Thereby the Pope was eliminated from the English Church.

The abrupt vanishing of the giant's body after the head was cut off signifies, I should think, the abrupt end of

---

[1] Observe that when one of the heads of the beast in Revelation (xiii, 3) is wounded, the deadly wound is healed; Spenser does not employ this detail, because inept.

Catholic prestige in England. By Duessa's casting her golden cup upon the ground and throwing her miter aside must be meant the refusal of Mary's bishops to accept the new order, which dissension followed close upon the Acts of Uniformity and Supremacy; and by the stripping Duessa of her gaudy clothes, the simplification of ecclesiastical robes. The rich interior of Orgoglio's castle refers to the rich furnishings and relics of the churches, and the blood upon the floors to the blood of martyrs, or of babes who had been sacrificed to the lust of monastic fathers and mothers.[1] Canto IX concludes with the adventure of St. George in the cave of Despair. I can see no political significance in this episode, and incline to regard it as one of the "purple patches." I believe that it simply illustrates the reactionary discouragement which followed upon the overthrow of Roman Catholicism.

In Canto X the Red Cross Knight is conducted by Una to the house of Holiness. The knight is welcomed by Cælia, and instructed in Christian duty by her daughters, Fidelia, Speranza, and Charissa. Patience then disciplines the knight, and Mercy conducts him through the hospital of Good Works. He is then prepared to climb with Una the hill of Contemplation and obtain a view of the city of Heaven.

This I take to be an allegorical picture of the growth of the English Church, or St. George, in the knowledge and discipline of Christianity. It refers to the spiritual training which the national Church enjoyed after the chains of Roman Catholicism were broken. It is general, rather than particular, in reference.

[1] On children's skulls found in monasteries, see Pilkington, Works, p. 687 [Parker Society].

In Canto XI Una conducts the Red Cross Knight to the brazen tower in which her parents are imprisoned. As the rescuers approach, they hear a hideous sound and behold the dragon stretched "upon the sunny side of a great hill." The knight bids Una retire, and prepares for the conflict.

At this point Spenser interrupts the narrative to appeal again to the Muse. The appeal is significant, as showing that the present episode is not military in reference, and that it is reserved for a future book to treat of the struggle with Spain. I make note of this because of the common assumption that in some vague way Book I has to do with England's foreign wars. In Book I Spenser strictly confines himself to the ecclesiastical struggle and is at pains to tell us so. The appeal is as follows:

> Now, O thou sacred Muse! most learned Dame,
> Fayre ympe of Phœbus and his aged bryde,
> The Nourse of time and everlasting fame,
> That warlike handes ennoblest with immortall name;
>
> O! gently come into my feeble brest;
> Come gently, but not with that mightie rage,
> Wherewith the martiall troupes thou doest infest,
> And hartes of great Heroës doest enrage,
> That nought their kindled corage may aswage:
> Soone as they dreadfull trompe begins to sownd,
> The God of warre with his fiers equipage
> Thou doest awake, sleepe never he so sownd;
> And scared nations doest with horror sterne astownd.
>
> Fayre Goddesse, lay that furious fitt asyde,
> Till I of warres and bloody Mars doe sing,
> And Bryton fieldes with Sarazin blood bedyde,
> Twixt that great faery Queene and Paynim king,
> That with their horror heven and earth did ring;

> A worke of labour long, and endlesse prayse:
> But now a while lett downe that haughtie string,
> And to my tunes thy second tenor rayse,
> That I this man of God his godly armes may blaze.

The dragon is very large and terrible, and disports himself with joy at the sight of a new victim. In the first day's battle the knight is early snatched up by the dragon and carried a long way through the air. But when the dragon at length sets him down from weariness, with his good spear the knight wounds his adversary under the left wing. Thereafter the knight has the best of it until the dragon, enraged that he cannot fly, breathes forth fire and then strikes the knight to the ground with his tail. The dragon leaves the knight for dead, but, as good fortune will have it, the knight falls backward into a well "full of great vertues." Before the dragon came to pollute it, this was known as "the well of life," and even now it has some virtue.

> For unto life the dead it could restore,
> And guilt of sinfull crimes cleane wash away;
> Those that with sicknesse were infected sore
> It could recure; and aged long decay
> Renew, as one were borne that very day.
> Both Silo this, and Jordan, did excell,
> And th' English Bath, and eke the German Spau;
> Ne can Cephise, nor Hebrus, match this well.

On the second day the knight first wounds the dragon, and then the monster, enraged, stings him with his tail, so that the sting goes through his shield and into his shoulder. The knight writhes with pain, yet, mindful of his honor, cuts off a portion of the tail. Thereupon the dragon leaps upon his shield. Unable to wrench it away, the knight resorts to his sword and severs a paw, which is left hanging upon the shield. Then the maddened dragon ends the day's conflict by again breathing forth fire and smoke.[1] This time the knight falls beneath "the tree of life," whose flowing balm heals his wounds.

On the third day the dragon rushes at the knight with intent to swallow him, but the knight runs his sword into the monster's vitals and kills him.

In this canto is depicted, I believe, the last great chapter in the conflict with Roman Catholicism, — a chapter that centers about the dramatic figure of Mary Queen of Scots. With its conclusion an inseparable barrier was erected between England and Rome, and England's ecclesiastical policy was unalterably defined.

Hardly had the Act of Supremacy been passed, before the clouds began to gather to the North, and for eleven years Elizabeth was harassed by the ambitious intrigues of Mary, who coveted the throne for herself and the Church for Rome.

It is needless to review at any length the details of this royal game of chess, which was begun with the landing of the French force at Leith and concluded only with the removal of Mary. After more or less intermittent trouble from 1559 to 1568, in which period England had once been drawn into actual military conflict, Mary suddenly assumed a more aggressive attitude and formed a coalition with certain powerful English families, looking toward coöperation with Spain in the unseating of Elizabeth. Aroused by her danger, Elizabeth quickly abandoned her policy of delay, and struck hard: Norfolk, as

[1] For a discussion of the allegorical meaning of "the well of life" and of "the tree of life" as Baptism and the Lord's Supper, cf. R. E. Neil Dodge, "The Well of Life and the Tree of Life," *Modern Philology*, Vol. VI, pp. 191–196.

leader, was sent to the Tower, and Mary was turned over to Lord Huntingdon, virtually a prisoner. These developments in England were watched by Rome with acute interest, and at the critical moment the Pope lent his powerful influence to the Roman Catholic cause by announcing that the Bull of Deposition was ready. Encouraged by this news, the Earls of Northumberland and Westmoreland in 1569 led the northern provinces in rebellion against Elizabeth. For a short time the rebellion promised to be successful, but the energy of Sussex was able to quell it. The next move of the Pope was to issue in the following year the Bull of Excommunication and Deposition, which a second time gave heart to the Roman Catholic sympathizers. In 1571 Norfolk, who had been released, again entered into an intrigue with Mary, supported by many lords of "the old blood," to secure the assistance of Spain in furthering a marriage of himself and Mary, and a subsequent assumption of the throne. The rumor of this project aroused Parliament to pass a series of extreme measures: the introduction of papal bulls into the country was declared high treason; an act of attainder was issued against the Northern earls; by the obligation of subscribing to the Articles of Faith, Roman Catholics were virtually debarred from all public office; and any person laying claim to the crown during the queen's lifetime was declared incapable of succeeding to it. The final scene was forthwith enacted, when the complete discovery of Norfolk's treason brought him and Northumberland to the scaffold and placed Mary in close confinement. Thus ended the last great conflict with Roman Catholicism.

To the advocates of the national Church these were years of gravest anxiety, for they recognized the tremendous significance of the outcome. The letters of the English reformers to their friends in Switzerland give the best evidence of the feelings of these contemporary Churchmen. Under date of August 7, 1570, Jewel writes to Bullinger:

> Antichrist seems now to have ventured his last cast, and to have thrown the world into confusion by seditions, tumults, wars, fury, fire, and flame. He perceives that it is now all over with him, and that destruction and death are impending over him and his party; so that his wretched object now is, not to perish ignobly or obscurely. Let the remembrance of them perish then with a noise.[1]

He then proceeds to write of the Proclamations of Northumberland and Westmoreland, of Bibles committed to the flames and masses performed, and proposes to send a copy of the bull, that Bullinger may see how "the beast is now raging." On August 8, 1571, Horn writes to Bullinger:

> Our government has been for almost the last three years in a dangerous and dreadful state of agitation; being not only shaken abroad by the perfidious attacks of our enemies, but troubled and disturbed at home by internal commotions. Both these kinds of pestilence, as is always the case, are the brood and offspring of popery, that pernicious and accursed fury of the whole world. But our noble and excellent virgin (queen), reposing in security at home, has broken both their forces at the same time, and destroyed the one without difficulty, and the other without bloodshed. Everything turned out so unexpectedly as it were from above, that it seemed as though the Lord of hosts and of might had undertaken from his heaven the cause of his gospel, and had fought, as it were, with his own hands.[2]

As a young and fervent Churchman, Spenser must have felt keenly the anxieties of these crucial days, and must have shared in the popular feeling at the end of the

---

[1] Zurich Letters, Vol. I, p. 227.
[2] Ibid. pp. 246–247.

struggle, that the final overthrow of Antichrist in England was divinely achieved. Certainly it is highly improbable that he would have left this important contemporary history out of his allegory of the English Church.

It is a question to what extent the details of the struggle between the knight and the dragon are to be applied to specific historical occurrences. The journey through the air may refer to the Northern rebellion; the sting which the dragon inflicts, to the papal bull; the cutting off of the tail, to the queen's retaliatory proclamation; the ruthless paw laid upon the shield, to Norfolk's intrigue to become king; and the cutting off of the paw, to the execution of Norfolk; but it is probably wiser not to attempt to follow the analogy too closely.

In the final canto the parents of Una, attended by a great throng, come forth rejoicing at their deliverance from the dragon. The knight and Una are conducted to the palace, and Una is promised to the knight. Just as the marriage ceremony is to be performed, a messenger rushes in and presents a letter from Fidessa, claiming that the knight is already plighted to her. The Red Cross Knight and Una in turn expose the falsehood of Duessa, and identify the crafty messenger as Archimago. The unfortunate man is bound and laid full low in a dungeon, and a guard placed over him, lest by his subtlety he should escape. The marriage is then consummated amid great rejoicing.

Here is poetically expressed the union of England and true religion. The truth once veiled is now fully revealed. England has achieved her divine mission of discovering the truth and is henceforth to be its defender. The letter of Duessa is of twofold meaning, — the Roman Catholic claim to England, and Mary Stuart's claim to the throne. This identification of Mary with Duessa is substantiated by Book V, Canto ix, where Duessa is tried before Mercilla. There Spenser has condensed into a few stanzas the whole case for and against the unfortunate queen. Wisdom, Kingdomes Care, Authority, Law of Nations, Religion, and Justice all inform against her, while Pittie, Regard of Womanhead, Daunger, Nobilitie of Birth, and Griefe plead for her. Zele shows that Duessa is in league with Ate, and produces Murder, Sedition, Incontinence, Adulterie, and lewd Impietie to acknowledge her as accomplice.[1] The ruthless handling of Archimago represents the extreme measures which were taken to suppress the Roman Catholics.

Such, in fine, I conceive to be the political and ecclesiastical allegory of this interesting book. I have of necessity worked in the realm of conjecture: if my conclusions meet with the favor of scholars, the task will have seemed doubly worth while; if my conclusions are refuted, I shall yet comfort myself with the joy of the effort and with the consciousness of the many new lines of interest that the task has opened to me.

[1] The reader should compare this passage with the charges preferred against Mary by Parliament in May, 1862: "The Bardon Papers," Camden Third Series, Vol. XVII, pp. 113 ff.

INDEX

Act of Supremacy, symbolically represented, 50.
Act of Uniformity, symbolically represented, 50.
Antichrist, identical with the Apocalyptic beast, 44; identical with the whole body of Papists, 44; symbolized by Orgoglio, 47.
Apocalypse, imagery of Duessa borrowed from harlot of, 42-43; citation from Bale's exposition of, 43; seven-headed beast adapted from beast of, 44; cited, 43, 44, 45, 48.
Arber, Edward, "An English Garner" cited, 35.
Archimago, symbol of Roman Catholic Church, 25, 58.
Ariosto, "Orlando Furioso" cited, 34.
Arthur, Prince, identified with "Magnificence," 46; symbolizes politically the national spirit of England, 46; symbolizes spiritually heavenly grace, 47.

Bale, Bishop, harlot of Apocalypse interpreted by, 43; writings of, cited, 44, 49.
"Bardon Papers, The," cited, 58.
Beast, seven-headed, adapted from beast of Apocalypse, 44-45; heads variously interpreted, 44.
Beast of Apocalypse, variously interpreted, 44.
Bible, symbolized by the horn of Arthur's squire, 48.
Blatant Beast, allegorical interpretation of, 8-9.
Book of Common Prayer, symbolized by book given to Arthur by the knight, 47-48.

Box, diamond, wine of Communion service represented by, 47.
Bull of Deposition, allegorically represented, 55-57.
Bullinger, Henry, letters to, 27-28, 56.

Canto I, outline of, 12-15; allegory of, discussed, 15-17, 25-28.
Canto II, outline of, 12-15; allegory of, discussed, 15, 25-28.
Canto III, outline of, 17-19; allegory of, discussed, 19-25.
Canto IV, outline of, 28-29; allegory of, discussed, 29-30.
Canto V, outline of, 28-29; allegory of, discussed, 29-30.
Canto VI, outline of, 30-31; allegory of, discussed, 31-36.
Canto VII, outline of, 36-39; allegory of, discussed, 42-51.
Canto VIII, outline of, 39-41; allegory of, discussed, 42-51.
Canto IX, outline of, 41-42; allegory of, discussed, 47-48.
Canto X, outline of, 51; allegory of, discussed, 51.
Canto XI, outline of, 52-54; allegory of, discussed, 54-57.
Canto XII, outline of, 57; allegory of, discussed, 57-58.
"Cantos of Mutabilitie" cited, 10.
Cave of Despair, a "purple patch," 51.
Church, English, growth of, allegorically represented, 51.
Church, Low, favored by Grindal, 7-8; favored by Spenser, 7-9; policy of, 28.
Clergy, reform, symbolized by Prince Arthur's squire, 48.
Clio, why addressed by poet, 3.

Cox, Bishop, in what sense a Puritan, 6.
Cranmer, Archbishop, writings of, cited, 6; allegorically represented by Sir Satyrane (?), 32–35; successor to Cromwell, 32–33; relation to Gardiner, 32–33; Foxe's estimate of, 33–34; youthful training of, 34.
Cromwell, Thomas, represented by the lion, 20-21; how regarded by contemporary Churchmen, 20–21.
Cup, Duessa's magic, identical with "cup full of abominations," 48.
Cup of abominations, how interpreted, 49.

Deposition, *see* Bull of Deposition.
Despair, *see* Cave of Despair.
Doyle, "Official Baronage of England" cited, 21.
Duessa, identified, as spirit of falsehood, with Roman Catholic Church, 25, 26, 29–30, 42, 46; as false living, 42; imagery of, borrowed from harlot of Apocalypse, 42–43; identified with Mary Queen of Scots, 54–58; letter of, explained, 57–58.
Dwarf, significance of, undetermined, 28.

Elissa, symbol of Puritanism, 10.
Elizabeth, Queen, identical with Faerie Queene, 3; identical with Belphœbe, 3; Bible kissed by, 4; remark of, on death of Mary Stuart, 50.
England, symbolized by St. George, 17; distinctive office of, 17; union of, with true religion, symbolized, 57.

"Faerie Queene," composition of, when begun, 4.
Foxe, John, vogue of his "Actes and Monuments," 4; estimate of Cromwell by, 20–21; estimate of Gardiner by, 22–23, 24; estimate of Cranmer by, 32–34;

"Actes and Monuments" cited, 20, 22, 24, 26, 27, 32, 33, 34, 35.

Gardiner, Stephen, represented by Sansloy, 22–23; Foxe's estimate of, 22–23, 24; Hall's estimate of, 23; Strype's estimate of, 23; relation of, to Cromwell, 22, 24; relation of, to Wolsey, 25; relation of, to Cranmer, 32–34.
Germany, symbolized by young squire (?), 26–27.
Grindal, Archbishop, identical with Algrind, 5; in what sense a Puritan, 7–8; letters of, to Henry Bullinger, 7, 28; letter of, to Rudolph Gualter, 7; Lutherans, how regarded by, 28.
Grosart, "Works of Spenser" cited, 4, 5.
Gualter, Rudolph, letter from Grindal to, 7; letter from Horn to, 27.

Hall, Edward, "Chronicle" cited, 23.
Harvey, Gabriel, letter to, 4; identical with Hobbinol, 5.
Henry VIII, identified with Red Cross Knight, 15–17, 26, 29, 42; not identical with the lion, 19.
Hoffmann, Max, dissertation of, cited, 2.
Holiness, house of, allegorically interpreted, 51.
Hooper, Bishop, writings of, cited, 6, 43.
Horn, Bishop, writings of, cited, 6, 8; Lutherans, how regarded by, 27; letter to Bullinger from, 56.
Horn, squire's, symbol of Bible, 48.

Insurrection in the West, symbolically represented, 49.

Jewel, Bishop, writings of, cited, 6; letter to Bullinger from, 56.
Jonson, Ben, interpretation of Blatant Beast by, 9.

Kirkrapine, significance of, 21–22.

Latimer, Hugh, discussion of, as Sir Satyrane, 35–36 (note 2).
"Life and Death of Thomas, Lord Cromwell," cited, 23.
Lion, the, wrongly identified with Henry VIII, 19; identified with Cromwell, 20–21.
Lutheranism, counterpart of "deceiving image" (?), 26–27; how regarded by English Churchmen, 27–28.

Martyrdoms, allegorically represented, 49–50.
Mary Queen of Scots, identified with Duessa, 54–58; Elizabeth's struggle with, allegorically represented, 54–58.
Mary Stuart, death of, allegorically represented, 50.
Mass, suppression of, allegorically represented, 48.
Medina, symbol of Low Churchmanship, 10.
Monasteries, suppression of, allegorically represented, 19–22.
"Mother Hubberd's Tale," cited, 10.

Norfolk, intrigue of, allegorically represented, 55.
Northumberland, see Proclamations of Northumberland and Westmoreland.

Orgoglio, symbol of power of Rome, 46; ancestry of, interpreted, 46.

Padelford, F. M., "Early Sixteenth Century Lyrics" cited, 21.
Parker, Archbishop, writings of, cited, 9.
Perissa, symbol of Roman Catholic Church, 10.
Pilkington, Bishop, writings of, cited, 51.
Platonism, Spenser's sympathy with, 11.
Pole, Cardinal, represented by Sansjoy (?), 30.

Pope, the, identical with Apocalyptic beast, 44.
Pride, household of, a "purple patch." 29.
Proclamations of Northumberland and Westmoreland, symbolically represented, 56–57.
Puritanism, extremes of, discussed, 6–11; Blatant Beast symbol of, 9; caricatured in "Cantos of Mutabilitie," 10; Elissa, symbol of. 10.

Raleigh, Sir Walter, Spenser's letter to, cited, 2, 46.
Rebellion in the North, symbolically represented, 55–57.
Red Cross Knight, symbol of St. George, or England, 15–17; identified with Henry VIII, 15–17, 26, 29.
Revelation, see Apocalypse.
Ridley, Bishop, writings of, cited, 6, 19, 35, 43, 44; cup of abominations interpreted by, 49.
Roman Catholic Church, clergy of, contrasted with Protestant, 5–6; allegorically represented by Perissa, 10; allegorically represented by Duessa, 25, 26, 29–30, 42, 43; deckings of, condemned by Bale, 43; struggle against, symbolized by conflict with Orgoglio, 46, 51; deckings of, allegorically represented, 51; final struggle against, symbolized by conflict with dragon, 54.
Rome, symbolized by harlot of Apocalypse, 44; doctrines of, symbolized by Duessa, 46; dominion of, symbolized by beast, 46; power of, symbolized by Orgoglio, 46.

St. George, symbol of England, 17.
Sandys, Archbishop, writings of, cited, 45.
Sansfoy, identified with Cardinal Wolsey, 25–26.
Sansjoy, identified with Cardinal Pole (?), 30.

Sansloy, identified with Bishop Gardiner, 22-23.
Satyrane, Sir, identified with Archbishop Cranmer (?), 32-35; possible identification with Latimer discussed, 35-36.
Scott, Sir Walter, editors of Spenser criticized by, 1.
Shepheardes Calender, ecclesiastical significance of, 5.
Shield of Prince Arthur, symbol of reform clergy, 48.
Spenser, Edmund, ecclesiastical sympathies of, 4-11; in what sense a Puritan, 6-11; early impressions of, 4; lover of the golden mean, 10-11; Platonism of, 11.
Squire (of Canto II), may symbolize Germany, 26-27.
Strype, "Life of Grindal" cited, 8; "Ecclesiastical Memorials" cited, 21, 23, 26; "Memorials of Archbishop Cranmer" cited, 34.

Tree of life, meaning of, 54 (note).
Turner, Dean, Lutherans how regarded by, 27-28.

Una, type of truth and true Church, 16, 47.
Upton, John, on allegory of Red Cross Knight, 2; on allegory of the lion, 19.

Van Dyke, Paul, "Renaissance Portraits" cited, 20.
Vander Noodt, Johan, identical with Diggon Davie, 5.

Well of life, meaning of, 54 (note).
Westmoreland, *see* Proclamations of Northumberland and Westmoreland.
Whitney, J. Ernest, on political allegory of "Faerie Queene," 1; quoted, 15-17.
Winstanley, Lilian, definition of Spenser's Puritanism and Platonism, 11; "Edmund Spenser: The Fowre Hymnes," cited, 11.
Wolsey, Cardinal, symbolized by Sansfoy, 25-26; relation to Gardiner, 25-26.

Zurich Letters, cited, 6, 7, 8, 9, 27.